Impulsive Sales:
How to sell on demonstration carts & kiosks

AMIR COHEN

Introduction

Ask almost anyone, and they'll tell you that working at a mall means a temporary, dead-end job making minimum wage or pitiful commissions. A salesman with high aspirations isn't likely to go seeking out a mall job for his income. Few outsiders are aware of how much revenue is generated, every single day, in a particular sector of mall jobs – the carts and kiosks industry.

A cart, or kiosk, is a small and usually mobile booth in a mall's common area, between the stores, where sales usually rely a great deal on impulse buying. Commonly these are what we call "static" carts; they display eye-catching and relatively affordable merchandise (like jewelry or cell phone accessories) while the salesman passively allows customers to approach the cart on their own.

A second type of cart is the "demonstration" cart, where the salesman approaches potential customers with a much more interactive method of showing and selling their products. This technique can be studied, learned, and profited from by anyone with the willingness to practice and the drive to make money.

This guide will teach you, start to finish, the technique to successfully sell on demonstration carts.

Demonstration cart sales can mean big bucks. It's not uncommon for people to make 10k-15k a month from working these booths, and even more during the holidays. I myself made those amounts, and I still have several friends who are doing the same. The high commissions, strategically ideal location, and dynamic work environment characteristics of demonstration carts give any salesman the opportunity for some very impressive profits.

Your cart has the most visibility. Everyone passing by sees it and sees what you have to offer. More importantly, though, they see **you**. Your job is to interact with them and, using your charm and sales technique, convince them make an impulsive purchase.

Despite the multitude of how-to books on sales, none cover the topic of how to sell to an impulsive customer. Or to be more precise, how to create an impulsive customer out of an unsuspecting one, sell them, and then make them buy even more. It might be a shock to some, but a single cart transaction can very often be hundreds or thousands of dollars – right there and then, on impulse, due to a fine sales job.

What's exciting about impulsive sales is that they revolve around the salesman himself. There's no marketing, signs or commercials - only the salesman and blank slate customers. You are the one in control; you don't need to depend on anyone or anything else to make your sale.

Impulsive sales are based on the most basic principles of the profession, and learning how to do it right means knowing how to sell. Period. Door-to-door, cold calling, car dealerships, or of course, the easy retail kind - the salesman who has mastered impulsive sales already knows how to do it all.

Salesmen from other fields who try to transfer to cart sales will usually discover that their old sales technique is not quite comprehensive enough. Depending on which field you came from, you might have to make minor adjustments, or you might have to relearn your entire technique. Working in Abercrombie does not make you a salesman. Learning the technique for cart sales, on the other hand, does.

So why is there so little information available about this lucrative field?

Simply put, it's still new. While cart sales have been around in some form or another for at least a couple decades, only recently has it become an acknowledged profession. When cart sales started, it was just regular people who really wanted to make money and were willing to give their all to do it. The field is still dominated by that kind of people - except now it's a billion dollar industry, if not more, and it's growing fast.

The type of salesmanship required when working on a cart combines the art of product demonstration used by sales artists, like Ron "Ronco" Popeil and Billie Mays, with the haggling skills, motivation and hunger of a flea market hustler. This might sound like a weird combination at first, but these are the skills we use for this unique, one-on-one, close-driven type of sales.

In this guide you will learn all about the different stages of an impulsive sale and how to master each of them.

The principles you will learn here are universal and can be applied to selling in any demonstration cart, but please remember this: know your product! Know every pitch, every objection, every application and then some. The more you know about your product, the better you can put to good use the principles you will learn here.

This guide is intentionally short and to the point. Don't expect 300 pages of stories and examples you'll never be able to read or memorize. You will not hear any worn-out sales phrases such as: K.I.S.S. (Keep It Simple Stupid), "Telling is not selling" or A.B.C (Always Be Closing). This is not a motivational guide, either. Rather, the chapters are kept short, concise and informational, with a narrow focus – namely, mastering the technique of impulsive sales. You should use this guide to study now and then refer to it in the future, while working on the cart, to criticize and improve your technique. Even the most experienced salesman gains benefit from going over these principles again and organizing their sales process. Even me.

Keep in mind, this guide is comprehensive, but it only covers the first step in becoming a great salesman: the basics. After you've mastered the principles in this guide, you'll be able to advance to personalizing the technique and make it your own.

There's a lot of information here. Try to keep up!

Let's begin.

Selling to the Unsuspecting Customer

First let's try to understand a little bit about our customers and what it is we're trying to do here.

Our job is to sell to the unsuspecting customer: the customer that is just walking around the mall, not expecting to buy or to even know about our product. We will sell to this guy. This is what we do, and this is what you will learn to do, too.

This type of sales is 90% up to the salesperson and only 10% up to the customer, so make sure you do it right. Your best ally and your worst enemy during this whole process is your own mind.

In order to make sales of this sort we have to choose a potential customer and guide that customer through the four stages of a cart sale: Stopping, Pitching, Closing, Up-selling.

Our customer is a person walking in the mall.

People come to the mall to shop. Our customers are all already there, waiting to be sold to. They came willing to spend money on things they like. They did not leave their wallets at home, and they didn't come to see the paintings on the walls. Their minds are preset to the idea of spending money. Now it's our job to show them something they like. A certain percentage of people in the USA (1%-5%, depending on where you are) will buy anything you show them. You can usually identify them easily; they will be holding bags from other demonstration carts. But we don't count on them; we just do our job the best way we can – we sell.

Customers will always reflect us, so it is important to always have the right approach to the sale. This is the principle of "**reflection**." If we are confident, they will listen to us; if we are stressed, they will be stressed; and if we enjoy selling to them, they will enjoy being sold to.

Step 1: Stopping

Stopping is the process of approaching a person walking near your cart and getting him to watch your demonstration or raising his interest in your product.

With some products, stopping is required to make the sale, and with other products, it just helps.

Here is the process for stopping people:

1. Never miss a potential customer walking by. A customer you didn't stop is a customer you didn't sell to. **Always be watching for potential customers**.

2. **Pick a target from the crowd** according to your product's criteria (e.g. Women, rich people, families with kids, everybody, etc.).

3. Before you approach the customer, **visualize them buying from you**. People will come to you when you are already seeing and feeling a good interaction with them. The sale happens in your head long before it happens at the register.

4. People don't like to feel they are being hawked - don't let the customer see you waiting for them, or they will decide to say no to you regardless of what you have to offer. **Approach the customer unnoticed**.

5. **Say your stopping phrase.** (e.g: "May I ask you a question?" or "Would you like a free [something]?")

Tip: Smile.

If a customer did not stop, we will withdraw pleasantly with a friendly "Have a nice day!" to keep good relations. We can stop him again the next time around.

Why would a customer stop?

A seemingly logical answer to this question is "because they are interested in the product." That is not the case. The customers don't know anything about the product until they actually try it. The product itself, its capabilities, and its price have very little to do with whether or not a customer stops.

Customers will stop because the salesperson or the way that they were approached seemed interesting to them. If a person is walking around the mall, shopping, and you approach to show them something interesting, why wouldn't they stop?

Don't be mechanical or robotic. People like to feel special and interesting. If people feel you didn't make an effort to stop them, or they feel that you're just using the same stopping phrase and the same approach over and over again that you've been using for the past five hours to the hundreds of people that walked there before them, they won't want to stop and talk to you. Spice things up. Be interesting. Treat every customer like he's the only one you care about – he is.

Tip: To stop more people, have fun stopping people! Treat it like a challenge and be playful.

Summary

For the perfect approach:

1. **Always be watching for potential customers**
2. **Pick a target from the crowd**
3. **Visualize them buying from you**
4. **Approach them unnoticed**
5. **Say your stopping phrase**
6. **Smile and have fun!**

Step 2: Pitching

Pitching is the art of demonstrating or showing a product in a way that makes the customer buy it on the spot.

For the perfect pitch, you will follow the C.A.B.A.S.A.K (by order of importance) or B.A.C.K-A.A.S (easier to remember) rules:

1. Control – Always be in control of the sale. You set the rhythm, pace, position and order of the demonstration, not the customer. If you will lead the customer, he will follow you – all the way to the register.

2. Assume a sale – Going into the demonstration you must assume a sale will be made at the end of it. You must have confidence that once the customer understands what the product can do for him, and once he hears how cheap the price is for such a product, then he will buy from you. If you treat the customer as a buyer, he will buy.

3. Be sharp – Talk fast and precise. Never lose rhythm.

4. Act confident – When demonstrating, your body language will set the customer's opinion of you. Feeling and acting confident, even a little cocky at times, increases his interest in you and what you're selling and will lower his ability to resist you. Keep eye contact, walk in a confident manner, and make decisive movements as well as hand gestures.

5. Show knowledge – While pitching, make sure to throw in bits of information, even when they're irrelevant or unimportant. Providing knowledge shows professionalism, and that's the kind of person a customer wants to buy from.

6. Answer every question – Customers will try to tackle you, look for your weakness, and find a reason why they shouldn't trust you or buy from you. Don't let them. Always respond to their questions and tackles quickly and precisely.

7. Keep the customer attentive – Make sure that the customer's eyes and focus are on you at all times. This will make him feel that he is part of the demonstration and that he is active. Ask questions, move around, and use your hands and body when you speak.

Bonding

This is a very important part when pitching one-on-one, like we do. Bonding with a customer can make or break a sale. Making a good connection with the customer can work to our benefit to the extent that some people will buy only because they like you so much.

The effects of bonding

Customers expect the process of buying a product to be a cold experience, where they are completely in control. Giving them a different experience baffles them and puts them in a new place, one where they want to buy from this person. It doesn't matter what he is selling – they love it!

When a customer thinks fondly of you, he thinks fondly of the product. When a customer doesn't think fondly of you, he doesn't like what you are selling. If you are neutral in the customer's eye, then you're wasting a valuable resource – the influence you have over the sale.

Tip: You can check to see how much influence you have on the customer by saying you like a certain color or texture and watching to see if he picks the same. This knowledge can be useful later.

Is there such thing as "too much bonding"?

Yes, there is. If you bond too much with a customer, he will feel comfortable with you, perhaps so comfortable that he won't have a problem saying "no" to you. In his mind, you are friends – you're both enjoying the time you spend together. If your demonstration is getting to be too much fun, you have to remind the customer what he is here for: to buy products from you. You do this by keeping your own focus on the sale and on the close – you want his money, not his companionship, don't forget that – even when you do enjoy your time together.

Not too much, not too little – just enough to make them think positively of you, and just enough to make them uncomfortable to say 'no'.

How to do: "bonding"

To bond with a customer, you have to act differently from how the customer expects a salesman to act, making the customer feel you're more than just a salesman to him.

Bonding with a customer is easier than you might expect. All you need to do is tell a little bit about yourself, ask some personal questions, and joke around – and you've already broken most of the habits of that expected "cold sale experience."

Tip: You should enjoy this part, as it's just like meeting new people all day long.

Notes

If we are convincing enough, the customer will close himself and will declare his buying the product. You want to go into each pitch expecting just that.

Tip: We are here to get the money. Always look for the opportunity and take it when you can.

Summary

For the perfect pitch:

1. **Control**
2. **Assume a sale**
3. **Be sharp**
4. **Act confident**
5. **Show knowledge**

6. Answer every question

7. Keep the customer attentive

8. Bond with them!

Step 3: Closing a sale

Once you've established that the customer wants the product you sell, it's time to close the sale and get the money. If the customer likes the product and has the money for it, he will buy it for sure as long as you handle him correctly.

Haggling

Haggling is the process of negotiating with a customer over the price of the deal. Most of our customers will assume that the mall is not a place you can haggle in. We will use that to our advantage.

Each product has a minimum price that you can sell it for, but has no maximum – you can sell for any price so long as it's more that the allowed minimum.

To take advantage of this option, we will start with an offer that might sound reasonable to the customer but still a little high, and we then negotiate the price or give a discount if necessary.

Our goal is to get as much money from the sale as possible, so we will always start with our highest offer and try to close for as high as we can.

Remember: you will never sell the product for a higher price than your initial offer, so make sure you give a good one.

We will never let a customer leave without hearing the minimum price.

When you close a sale at a price that's above the minimum, you will almost certainly be able to "up-sell" the customer and sell him more products to increase the total sale amount. You will learn more about this in *Step 4: Up-selling*.

A good **haggle** will always include a reason to make the customer feel you are doing it especially for him. Give a good reason for lowering the price, and you will gain credibility. The more credible you are, the more the customer will be inclined to buy.

Customers don't like to buy from a place that lowers prices for no reason because it makes them feel that they are being scammed.

Some customers like to haggle. You will sell them when you will make them feel like they've won the haggling game. It's important to identify those people as soon as possible and let them feel they won, or you could lose the sale during the haggling process because they will demand a price that's lower than the minimum.

Handling objections

When a person is becoming convinced, he will naturally start to object. If no objections occur, it can be for one of two reasons: the customer is a sucker (excellent!) or the customer is not thinking about buying it (bad!). If there are no objections, you must identify quickly which type your customer is, or you may waste a lot of time.

Common techniques in handling objections

1. **Repeat the pitch** – means repeating parts or all of the pitch while speaking in a fast, passionate manner.

2. **Tempt** – means lowering the price "especially" for the customer.

3. **Tell a story/testimonial** – means telling a personal story, like a story that happens to another customer you had or someone you know, to emphasize a point.

4. **Rule it out** – means to "rule out" the customer's behavior, dismissing his objection wholly and emphatically, in an assertive way to make him think he acted rude or foolish.

Common objections and how to handle them

Price objection:

Price objections are divided into two categories: budget and value. Budget means "the price is more than I can realistically spend" and value means "the price does not justify what the product is doing for me."

Price objection, budget – Tempt.

Price objection, value – (1) Rule it out (2) Repeat the pitch (3) Tempt.

Salesman objections:

The customer has a problem with the selling process. Either he doesn't like to be sold to (ego resistance – he wants to be the one pulling the strings) or he doesn't like to buy on the spot (insecurity resistance – in his mind, impulsive equals stupid).

Salesman objections – Tell a story or testimonial.

Your story should make the customer feel better about being sold to (not manipulated, stupid, or foolish) and raise your credibility. Examples are describing a previous customer who ended up delighted and satisfied with his purchase or describing someone who passed up a discounted price and regretted it.

Trust objections:

Trust objections occur when the customer doesn't believe he can trust the salesman's claims.

Trust objections, the customer doesn't believe in you (that what you say is true) – (1) Rule it out (2) Repeat the pitch.

Trust objections, the customer doesn't believe in the product – Tell a story/testimonial to gain credibility.

If the customer believes you, likes the product, and has the money for it, then a sale should be made.

The best way to handle an objection is to identify it.

If the customer will not close and you haven't been able to identify the objection, then repeat the pitch until you identify the real objection.

The salesman's job is to turn a "no" into a "yes." If you can't turn a "no" into a "yes," then you're not selling, you're simple giving a presentation.

Remember: Assume a sale. Never give an offer without seeing a "yes" in your mind.

The 99 cents rule

Whenever you name a price, even if you're saying $10,000, you have to feel like you just said, "It's 99 cents."

By **reflection**, the customer will feel what you feel about the price. If you feel the price you're giving is high, the customer will also think the price is high, and won't buy from you; but if you feel the price you say is low then customer will also think the price is low, and will then buy. Whatever price you are saying, always imagine you just said the words: "It's just 99 cents."

Applying Pressure

Don't be afraid to be pushy or apply pressure to close the sale. Pressure helps most people make up their mind and say '"yes."

When should you apply pressure?

When you know that you have influence on the customer and that you can help them make up their mind.

When you believe you can push to close a sale without the customer getting "locked."

What is a "locked" customer?

A "locked" customer is a customer that felt too pressured and got locked in a "no" state of mind, after which he can't be convinced. If your customer is locked, the only way to have a chance in unlocking him is to make him feel there's no pressure involved at all and to prove to him that you are not trying to push him to buy. Avoid thisas soon as you see it coming with reassurances like: "it's ok, you don't have to buy," "no pressure here," or "of course you can always think about it and come back; we just want you to feel comfortable with the purchase."

Tip: There are no right or wrong motives for purchasing! When a customer buys, it doesn't matter if he bought it because of us, because he wants it, or because he feels bad for walking away empty handed.

Summary

For the perfect close:

1. Assume a sale.

2. Use the 99 cents rule.

3. Give an offer. If it's your first offer, give your highest offer. If it's not the first offer, haggle (give an excuse and a better offer).

4. Handle objections, if any.

5. Repeat the process three times until the sale is closed or you have given your best offer.

6. Apply pressure.

Step 4: Up-selling

Up-selling a customer means making a customer that already bought something from you buy more.

Up-selling is a very important part of making money in a cart. At this point, you will often be in a position where every sentence you say can increase your total sale amount and sometimes even double or triple it.

Up-selling begins once the customer has already agreed to purchase a product. There are two ways to do this:

1. <u>Show more products:</u>

   If you need to show more products, place the product the customer already agreed to buy at the register area to prevent the customer from buying the second product instead of the first and to prevent him from forgetting he was already closed.

   If the product is in the register area, in the customer's mind he has already bought it.

2. <u>Up-sell at the register:</u>

   If you don't need to show any more products, the up-selling will be made at the register while holding the customer's credit card (or any other payment method) in your hand.

If you successfully up-sell a customer by showing him more products, you will try to up-sell him again at the register.

Giving offers when up-selling

The total amount of the sale needs to be equal or higher to the sum of the minimum prices of the products sold. If you sold the first product above minimum price, then you can use your "extra" to sweeten the deal.

Extra – the different between the minimum price and your sale price. If the minimum price of product A is $100, and you sold it for $110, then you have $10 extra.

You can sell a product below the minimum price if you have an extra from another product you sold **in the same sale**. For example, if the minimum price of product A is $100, and you sold it for $110, you can then sell a second product A in the same sale for $90 because you have a $10 extra. The total amount will be $200 for two of product A, making it equal to the sum of the minimum prices of all the products sold.

Notice how we used a $10 extra to give the customer a $20 discount – a big difference and a big motivation to buy.

You will usually have several options to offer the customer when trying to up-sell him, so make sure you take note of all of them before you start your offers.

When using your extra to up-sell a customer, always start with the offer that will bring you the most money.

You do not have to use your entire extra on the first up-sell. You can use some of it and save some for the next up-sell.

When up-selling, every $5 or $1 extra is important because it can be used to make the customer buy another product.

When making an offer, always emphasize the product's value and benefit and not the price.

Feeling It

There's no easy formula for it, and there's no way around it: you have to learn to "feel" your customers. Every person has a certain degree of intuition, and a good salesman learns to trust his.

People send clues out to the environment about how they are feeling and what they want or need. Those clues, whether or not you realize it, are constantly being picked up by your subconscious. What you have to do now is listen to them. Begin learning to sense the unspoken clues in people's reactions to you and your product, and use those clues to judge what to do next: let go, press on, talk or act in a certain way, etc.

Luckily, intuition is something you were already born with. Your emotions and instinct in these cases are usually right. The part you have to learn is how to recognize the feeling, listen to it, and adjust yourself accordingly. You can't be a salesman without knowing how to feel the other side.

It's okay if you don't yet know how to listen to your intuition. Don't worry! It's simply a matter of practice. Like all new skills, practice makes perfect. Pay attention to your inner instincts as they occur. Notice the gut reaction you get about how to handle people. Notice how it felt when you were right, and notice how it felt when you were wrong. Even if you don't think you're "feeling it," just keep trying. Be willing to make mistakes, keep practicing, and eventually it **will** begin to click. The more you recognize and go with your intuition, the more natural and familiar it will become to you. You may find one day that it has become your most effective sales tool of all.

All the techniques described so far, once mastered, are the essential tools in your toolbox. You need to learn to use them and use them in the best way. Stay set on your goal – to sell, to make money. Remember the process you learned here, and then practice using it in context until you learn to naturally feel the situation at hand.

The Mindset

After mastering the four stages of a sale, Stopping, Pitching, Closing and Up-selling, there's one more thing you need to be a good salesman – you need to have the right mindset.

The correct mindset makes all the difference between good and bad salesmen.

Take note:

1. Good salesmen always push themselves; they never let themselves give up.

2. Good salesmen enjoy what they do. They always challenge themselves, and they always treat every day like it is a game and they're trying to score the most points.

3. Good salesmen understand that the sale is up to them. They know that there's no such thing as bad mall or bad people.

4. Good salesmen are always learning and trying to improve and know more about what they do.

And now, there's one more thing you should know. This is the secret of success – the one that guides all good salesmen.

The Secret of Success

The secret of success is a mindset that can be defined in a single mantra: Don't be a Fryer.

Definition of a Fryer:

1. A person who could have done better for himself, but didn't.

2. A person who is gullible and can be/has been taken advantage of, a "sucker."

   Examples:

   If you could have sold the product for $300, but you only sold it for $100 – you're a Fryer.

   If you could have sold 4 products, but you only sold 1 – you're a Fryer.

   If you could have stopped a customer and sold him, but you let someone else do it – you're a Fryer.

   If you're customer bought 3 products without asking for a deal, when he knows we give them – he's a Fryer.

If you're only going to remember one thing from this entire guide, please remember this:

Don't be a Fryer.

Rules of the Trade

Not everybody buys

It's very important to remember that. We see a lot of people every day, and we demonstrate a lot, but not everybody buys. Don't let it get you down. The harder you try, the more you'll sell.

No half demonstrations

> *Remember: You either do a demo, or you don't – you can't do both.*

You get to choose who you want to demonstrate for. That means that once you decided to do a demonstration, you have to do it right. Avoid the trap of thinking to yourself "Oh, he's probably not going to buy, so I'm not going to try that hard with him." If you stopped someone, if you chose to try and sell him, you have to follow it through – give it everything you got and do the best demo you can.

Be a positive influence

> *Remember: Negative people fail.*

Your hardest battle will not be with customers over sales, it will be with yourself and with the negativity of other people around you. Negativity can come from anyone. Never let anything stray you from your positive attitude during the day. Toxic people who have only bad things to say and who bring in negativity have no place around us. Don't let yourself start thinking bad thoughts when sales don't go well. Don't look for blame. Don't think badly about yourself. You're a salesperson, and sometimes you'll have bad days. The only way to change a bad day is to be positive and try harder.

Remember: One customer can change everything to the better.

Never let yourself think, "Oh, this is a bad day, so I'm not going to try that hard." You have to try hard, and you have to do it until the end. That's the professional salesperson's way of making the best paycheck he can for himself. And that's how we do things.

Tips & Tricks

1. Use superlatives.

Use words like "Amazing!" "Incredible!" and "Oh my God!" when selling a product. People need that to feel they are buying something special. You don't have to get excited yourself every time, but it is important to get them excited, and these words do the trick. That's what Steve Jobs does.

2. What happens once will happen again.

This is one of my favorites and one of the tricks I find most useful. Interestingly enough, it works in life just the same as in sales.

People have a certain way in which they become convinced. Some need pressure, and some need a minute to think. Some need superlatives screamed at them, and some just buy whatever they feel everybody else is buying. To some, a free gift makes a good deal, and to some, a discount makes a good deal.

Real life example:

The product's minimum is $50. I told the customer it cost $100 and gave him a "buy one, get one free" offer. He said no. I then haggled and eventually he agreed to buy for $50. When up-selling him, I offered him another one for "only $50!" and he said yes. He eventually bought 2 for $100; he just needed to hear it the right way.

If you managed to close a customer using one technique, it will work again if you use the same technique when you up-sell.

Other examples:

If you closed the sale by applying pressure, don't give them a minute when offering an up-sell – apply pressure!

If a person didn't want a discount, but bought because he got a free gift, don't offer them another product at a discount – offer them another product with another free gift!

If a person bought because he felt like a sucker not to, don't try to up-sell him with the benefits of the product – just make him feel like a sucker again if he doesn't buy.

I can go on forever with those examples, but hopefully you get the idea. Use what you've already seen works.

3. Exaggerating

When people hear a salesman sell, they automatically believe only about half of it and assume he's exaggerating. So if you want people to have the right idea about your product, you'll have to exaggerate. Everything you say needs to be spiced up with, "Chosen number one in the world!" or "You'll never need ... ever again!" If something lasts 3 or 4 months you will say, "It lasts a year!" – because if you actually say 3 months, they're just going to assume it runs out after a week.

4. The 1-0-5 trick

When haggling with a customer who likes to haggle, or with someone who likes to say the final word, it's usually best to let them feel they've won. A lot of times with these type of people you will find yourself in a situation in which you'll want to say something similar to "$100 and we have a deal?" and it will work more often than not, but from time to time the haggler will just say "make it $80!" in response. A better way to do it is to use the 1-0-5 trick.
When you feel you can close the deal for $100, instead of saying "$100 and we have a deal?" say, "$105 and we have a deal?" and watch the customer follow up with "make it $100!" and close the deal for you. This trick will also work with 155, 205, 255 and anything else that sounds like a "whole" number.

5. Stopping the "I have it" customers

People ask me many times what to say, or how to stop the customer that in response to our stopping phrase say "I have it!" but are lying to get away or really do have it but can still buy more.

There are 2 good ways to rebuttal the "I have it", which approach is best for you depends on your product. Consult your manager on what's the best way if you're not sure.

1. The "I don't care" approach

    Raise your hand in front of the customer, as if to say "stop", and say "Just for information, this is a new version" you can add superlatives like "only 2 weeks in the market!" or "it hasn't even come out yet!" and then just say "Let me show you!" and lead the customer by simply walking off to the cart.

2. The "Engaging" approach

    You can ask the customer engaging questions like "where did you get it?" and then follow with "which one?" walk off to the cart point at some random products and say "this one or this one?" Politeness dictates that they will follow you and answer your question. Once you got them talking you can continue the conversation and try to get them to try the products you want to demonstrate to them.

6. Dirty Tricks

Dirty tricks are called that because they will often sound morally gray at best. I'm not judging the morality of these tools, I'm just giving you the information objectively – you'll choose what to do with it.

6.1. Flirting

Flirting is just one of the forms of **bonding** and is not a dirty trick by itself. It means suggesting you may be interested in or attracted to the other person by using compliments, body language, etc.

You can easily use flirting to bond by giving out compliments and doing things that can be interpreted as showing interest (such as proximity, tone of voice, etc). If you manage to do this without being threatening, you'll be making the other person feel good and bonded with you – you broke all expectation of the sale experience being cold, and you did it in the most positive way possible.

Nothing dirty so far. But if, while flirting, you suggest that more can happen between you two, it will make the customer feel that not buying will ruin the atmosphere and will make them spend a little bit of money to satisfy the flirting process and see where it leads.

The reason I wouldn't recommend this dirty trick is because it usually just leads to dead-end small sales. Sometimes it can be what will help you take your mind out of a negative state, but generally speaking, you didn't learn everything you did to be doing this on a regular basis – that's just bad salesmanship.

6.2 "The Messed Up Box" Trick

Salesmen use a lot of innovative excuses to give the customer a lower price without sounding like a hustler. One dirty trick that is a favorite of mine is "The Messed Up Box" trick.

What you need to do is offer the customer the product in a package that was "messed up" in shipping and explain that's why you can't sell it for full price. You assure them that everything works fine, showing them it's not damaged from the inside, but because of the messed up package, they can get a huge discount.

This trick also works well because it creates urgency – the customer cannot wait or think about it because there is only one like this and when it's gone, it's gone. A lot of salesmen keep one messed up box somewhere on the cart and pull it out when necessary.

Etiquette for Working in a Cart

Keeping etiquette rules while selling on the cart will work to the benefit of everybody and will allow you a comfortable and supportive working environment.

You, as a salesman, are a part of a team.

> 1. Do not take other people's sales if they are at the location.
>
> 2. When stopping people, do not cross another salesman's way.
>
> 3. Do not speak with other salesmen's customers; do not stare or make eye contact with them.
>
> 4. Unless training a new salesman, do not interfere with another salesman's sale.
>
> 5. Keep prices private between you and your customers.

Appendix I: Up-Selling (Advanced)

When up-selling, you can show a product's value and benefit to the customer by tying it together to the product he already got and showing that they complete each other. Beware, however, of oversell.

What is Oversell?

Oversell is your worst enemy when up-selling. It is a situation where the customer gets the feeling that it's all or nothing and chooses nothing. In this situation, you lose the sale that has already been closed.

The best way to avoid oversell is to hold the customer's credit card in your hand before making the customer feel he can't buy product A without product B – and backing off if required.

Example:

You go to buy an ice cream from an ice-cream truck.

One ice cream scoop costs $5, 2 scoops cost $9, and 5 scoops cost $10.

You choose 2 scoops, because it's a better deal than only 1 scoop, and even though it's just $1 more for 5 scoops, that's just too much.

The ice-cream guy tries to sell you 5 scoops. He makes you feel like a sucker if you buy only 2 and not 5 because it's only $1 difference.

You really don't want 5, but you also don't want to feel like a sucker. So you walk away.

The ice-cream guy has lost the sale because of oversell.

If the ice-cream guy had taken your money before trying so hard, and backing off when not succeeding, he would have made a sale.

Oversell happens from time to time even to the best of salesmen. It's still worth trying to up-sell **every time**.

Techniques for up-selling:

1. Apply pressure.

2. Repeat the pitch.

3. Make him feel like a sucker – Give your offer in a way that will make much more sense to buy more than not to. Say something like, "You deserve to get another one for only XX..." Say that everybody is taking it. Be surprised and confused if he refuses: "Really? It's only XX more..." Do not use pressure when using this method.

4. Decide for him – You can make up his mind for him and order him to buy another product. "No, I don't want to hear about it, you are taking another one for your sister!" Only do this if you know you have a lot of influence over him. Be certain to get approval before swiping the card if using this method.

You stop trying to up-sell when you see customer's objections are becoming stronger and/or he is becoming locked. If the customer's objections are getting weaker, you must continue to try and close another product.

Appendix II: Selling to a Group

Selling to a group is great. You can sell two, three, four or even five sets of products while doing only one pitch. The general approach is to sell the most dominant member of the group (the leader) and make sure the rest follow.

How to identify the leader

The leader of your group will be its most dominant member, and that's the person who will make the final decision. You can identify him when you see other members of the group looking at him for permission; the dominant member is usually the first one to come up to you, and he usually makes the strongest impression (although this rule does not apply universally).

In general, when approaching to stop a group of people, if you stop the dominant member, they will all stop. Sometimes, though, that's not an option, either because you can't identify them or because they are not within your target crowd (e.g. the husband is the dominant, and the wife is the target). If this is the case, just approach the person who seems the easiest to stop and then handle objections, if any, from the dominant member of the group. A common trick you can use in this case is to tell the dominant member, "You'll be the judge." This makes him feel like he's participating and lowers his objection for a demo.

This phrase will also work whenever you want to make somebody feel included.

Don't feel obligated to address the "judge" as a "judge" again, unless it helps your sale.

When doing a demo to more than one person, you must always include and talk to everyone in the group. Make them all feel that they are participating – but always pay special attention to the dominant.

Large groups

When selling to a large group, the demonstration will always be conducted as if you are standing on a stage and putting on a show. Talk loud, pay attention to everyone, and make them laugh. It is very important to be very assertive and in control, or this could easily get out of hand. Don't be afraid to be bossy towards them sometimes (with a wink and a smile, of course). They don't expect that (which means it's both **bonding** and useful!).

Make sure everyone follows

After selling to a part of the group, assume a sale (in your head) while asking the other members in the group if they want one too in the most confident and nonchalant voice you have. Take what you got casually to the register and take the payment method (to avoid **oversell)**, and then try to up-sell the members of the group by using each other's purchases as peer-pressure to buy more ("Really, Mary? You don't want it to complete the set? Bob got it… and Suzanne too!").

Glossary

99-cent rule – The term for presenting a price while thinking "99 cents" at the same time to communicate solid confidence in the price.

B.A.C.K-A.A.S – See "C.A.B.A.S.A.K."

Bonding – Befriending a customer for the purpose of lowering his objections to the sale and raising his discomfort to refuse.

C.A.B.A.S.A.K – The initials of the 7 principles for a perfect pitch by order of importance: Control, Assume a sale, Be sharp, Act confident, Show knowledge, Answer every question, Keep the customer attentive.

Cart – A mobile booth in the mall common area.

Cart-sale – A sale that is being made on a cart or kiosk. These sales usually revolve around a "Wow" effect and include demonstration and haggling. To make a cart-sale you must follow the four steps of a cart-sale: Stopping, Pitching, Closing and Up-selling.

Closing – The 3rd step of a cart-sale. Once the customer wants the product we will handle objections and haggle to close the deal at the highest price.

Extra – The amount of dollars above minimum price of a sale. If product A's minimum price is $150, and Product B's minimum price is $50, and I sell product A and B for $220, I have $20 **extra.**

Flirting – A technique used for **bonding** which also can be done in a dirty way in order to close a sale.

Fryer – A person who lets other people do better than him, kind of like a "sucker." Don't be one! (See "The Mindset" for more definition).

Haggle – The process of arguing over the price in order to close the deal.

Kiosk – An immobile unit/structure in the mall common area.

"Locked" Customer – A customer that was pressured too much and is now stuck in saying "no" without considering the content of any offer.

Minimum Price – The lowest price the salesman is allowed to sell a product for.

Objections – What people feel when they are starting to become convinced. We must handle each of them and get them out of the way to close the deal.

Oversell – Putting the customer in a position where he feels it's "all or nothing" and chooses nothing.

Pitching – The 2nd step of a cart-sale. Pitching is the art of demonstrating a product with the purpose of selling in mind. Pitching on a cart follows the **C.A.B.A.S.A.K** (in order) / **B.A.C.K-A.A.S** (easy to remember) principles.

Pressure – One of the tools used to convince customers and close sales.

Price – The presented cost of the product. Usually negotiable.

Product – What we sell in a cart/kiosk. Usually has a "wow" effect.

Reflection – The principle that tells us that customers will reflect how we feel towards them and act the same way back to us.

Sale – Taking the money and giving the products; a.k.a. the goal of everything in this book.

Stopping – Usually the 1st step of a cart-sale, some products may skip this step. It is the process of approaching people in an interesting way for the purpose of bringing them to a demonstration and selling them the product.

Superlatives – Words used to create excitement in customer by making the product feel like the "most" or "best" of something (e.g. "Amazing!" "Oh my God!").

"The Messed Up Box" Trick – An excuse salesmen use to offer a lower price and create urgency. The trick involves a new product in a messed up box.

The Secret of Success – Don't be a Fryer.

Up-selling – The 4th step of a cart-sale. After closing the sale but before charging, we take the payment method and try to sell more.

Final words

Thanks for reading.

Now you know everything I've learned in my years of experience working on demonstration carts. I've tried to lay it all out in an easy to understand, straight to the point way. I hope this will help you get the most of your work experience and get you to make the tons of money you deserve to be making.

If you have any suggestions, comments or questions, you can contact me through e-mail:

Amir Cohen,
amcor2000@gmail.com

###

www.ingramcontent.com/pod-product-compliance
Lightning Source LLC
Chambersburg PA
CBHW071637170526
45166CB00003B/1354